We Are Still
Not Counted as Human

Reflections on the
Struggle for Dignity in South Africa

S'bu Zikode

Daraja Press

Published by
Daraja Press
https://darajapress.com
Wakefield, Quebec, Canada

© 2025 S'bu Zikode
Introduction and interview conducted by Richard Pithouse
ISBN: 978-1-997742-15-9

Book design by Kate McDonnell
Photo by Michael Premo

A short version of this interview was published in the *Boston Review*
(Pithouse, R. (2024) 'Repression is always a lesson: An interview with
S'bu Zikode', *Boston Review*, Spring. Available at: http://bit.ly/48pYO-
zI) and in the *Journal of Asian and African Studies* (Pithouse, R. (2025)
'"We are still not counted as human": Contesting unfreedom from below
in South Africa', *Journal of Asian and African Studies*, 60(2), pp. 1325–1345.
doi:10.1177/00219096241295637. Our thanks to the editors for permission to
make this complete interview available.

Abahlali baseMjondolo – residents of the shacks – is the largest popular movement to have emerged in South Africa after apartheid. Founded in Durban in 2005 it now – in September 2025 – has more than 180,000 members organised into more than 100 branches across four of South Africa's nine provinces.

In this interview with Richard Pithouse, S'bu Zikode, the President of Abahlali baseMjondolo, reflects on the three decades since Nelson Mandela ascended to the South African Presidency. Interviews were conducted on 4, 8, 19, 25, 26 and 27 March 2024.

A Window into Life in Struggle

Thirty-two people from twelve shack settlements attended a meeting in Durban on 4 October 2005, where the decision was made to establish Abahlali baseMjondolo. When the movement celebrated its twentieth anniversary at the historic Curries Fountain Stadium in Durban on 4 October 2025, it had more than 180,000 members in good standing, organised through over 100 branches across five of South Africa's nine provinces.

Abahlali baseMjondolo is, by far, the largest and best organized popular movement to have emerged in South Africa after apartheid. It has secured significant wins for its members, especially regarding land. It has also achieved some gains for impoverished people in general. It has endured and survived waves of severe repression, including organized slander, assaults, arrests, torture, imprisonment, and assassinations. It stands as one of the most important movements in the shanty towns, now home to more than a billion people across the planet.

Like similar movements worldwide, Abahlali baseMjondolo is woven from countless threads – each representing a person's choice to resist within a community. This interview with S'bu Zikode, a co-founder of the movement, its most innovative thinker during its early years, and its most prominent leader, follows one of those threads.

Emancipatory politics begins when those considered less than fully human within an oppressive system claim their equal humanity through thought, speech, and action. This can include asserting the right to transgress spatial boundaries. Such actions are often initially met with ridicule, the belief that agency must originate from external sources, infantilization, criminalization, and repression. If their voices are heard at all in the elite public sphere, it is usually only as noise or in fragments.

There is a long history, across place and time, of deep social and political suspicion of impoverished people living in cities – particularly when they live on occupied land or in occupied buildings, and make a living outside wage labour. This is always intensified when class intersects with race, caste or national status.

It is no surprise that liberal ways of understanding the world are systematically incapable of communicating much of the reality of struggles waged from the banlieues of Paris, the favelas of Rio, or the imijondolo of Durban. This is not just true of the forms of liberalism that tend to see grassroots militancy in criminal terms, or to see it as consequent to some sort of external conspiracy. It is also often true of the currents of liberalism that have some sympathy for grassroots activism. They frequently cast its protagonists as victims without real politics. This happens when, for instance, a militant who explicitly self-identified as communist and a Pan-Africanist, was committed to radical internationalism, took a leading role in building a commune on occupied land and established a radical reading group in a prison, is, after his assassination, presented as a 'human rights defender'.

For some, it may be surprising that leftist ways of understanding the world often also fail to grasp or communicate the realities of these kinds of struggles. It is not uncommon for the views of the middle-class left to be shaped more by assumptions than by thorough investigation. In South Africa, it is not unusual – from certain strands of academic Marxism to currents in trade unions, sections of the Palestine solidarity movement, and left-wing NGOs – for impoverished African people to be seen as lacking independent political capacity. This is often taken as an assumption of common sense, resulting in grassroots activists being ignored or even – as has happened – criminalized. They are frequently viewed as people to be bused in to fill seats at meetings or events organised by the middle class, rather than as individuals to be engaged with on the basis of equality. This infantilization can be profoundly racialized.

In elite publics, the socially accepted ways of interpreting the politics of impoverished urban communities often reflect the assumptions and biases of elites more than the actual experiences and perspectives of oppressed people involved in collective movements. This is further complicated by the fact that the most significant discussions in these movements are often expressed in languages that lack international reach and are more closely tied to specific places and times than elite forms of communication. They also tend to have a fleeting presence. An article published online might be accessible for years. An article in an academic journal may have a more or less permanent availability. This is not the case for a speech at a meeting, a voice note on a WhatsApp group, or a poem performed at a funeral.

All this poses challenges for people who wish to develop a meaningful understanding of a movement from a distance.

Movements are many things. They are an accumulation of experiences, practices, stories and meetings across space and time. There are many ways to develop and communicate a meaningful understanding of all this. One is to take some time out from the unremitting pressures of organizing on the terrain of constant crisis to record something of the arc of the lives and thinking of the protagonists in a movement. This interview traces the movement of one person's life into and through struggle.

Abahlali baseMjondolo was built from a wider national ferment among impoverished people that, beginning in Johannesburg in 2004, often took the form of road blockades with burning tyres. It was only in Durban that a movement was forged from this surge of protest. There are a number of reasons for this, but among the most significant was S'bu Zikode's leadership. There are also many reasons why the movement has not only survived for 20 years despite severe repression but has also grown. The moral authority generated through Zikode's mode of leadership is one of those reasons.

Zikode always affirms and receives the honours that come to him in the name of the movement, in the name of the people who are, together, a movement. Nonetheless, his significance in what has been achieved cannot be denied.

From the outset, his leadership was marked by impeccable personal integrity; a willingness to think freely and creatively from the present and into the future, rather than to repeat exhausted forms of politics; an axiomatic commitment to the immediate and universal recognition of the dignity of the oppressed; and a soft-spoken personal courage. He thought and spoke from within the language and culture of the people he led, drawing out its emancipatory possibilities — with respect for the personhood of all as the measure. He invited people into collective deliberation rather than obedience, listened more than he spoke, and when he spoke it was to weave consensus rather than to give a line. People who were profoundly dishonoured in the logic of oppression, including by national elites, were received with respect.

Expressed mainly in the language of African humanism, Zikode's politics resonates with the ethic at the heart of liberation theology, and with many aspects of Paulo Freire's thought. It is well captured in Freire's secular axiom that the oppressed "cannot enter the struggle as objects in order later to become human beings."[1]

South Africa is in a grave crisis, with mass unemployment and growing impoverishment and inequality. Aside from the remarkable support that the ruling party, the African National Congress, has given to Palestine, there is an almost complete lack of political imagination among the ruling class. There are powerful kleptocratic forces in and around the state, and as the ANC's electoral support rapidly collapses, a number of the parties moving to take the opening political space are authoritarian, corrupt and deeply xenophobic. There is, at the same time, an alarming shift to the right within society with pervasive xenophobia, strong support for extrajudicial police executions and growing attraction to authoritarian leaders.

If Abahlali baseMjondolo were ten times stronger, or if there were many similar movements, it would be able to mount a significant challenge to this. The movement has, on occasion, given national leadership, such as in July 2025 when it became the first and thus far only organization to confront and humiliate Operation Dudula – a militarised fascist group organized around extreme xenophobia.

1 Freire, P. (1970) *Pedagogy of the Oppressed*. London: Penguin Books. p. 50.

But it does not have the power to mount a systemic challenge to the growing attempts to impose authoritarian containment on the escalating social and political crisis.

But although the situation is grim, Abahlali baseMjondolo's impressive achievements show that there is no inevitability about the degeneration of South African politics and that it is possible to build principled and emancipatory forms of popular democratic power from below.

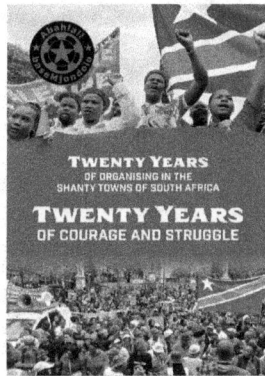

Readers should refer to *Abahlali baseMjondolo: Twenty years of courage and struggle* (http://bit.ly/4okEy7R), which presents the remarkable and richly detailed history of the shack dwellers movement in South Africa, chronicling two decades of its existence, persistence, and beauty of emancipation in rehearsal. The narrative details how they have built democratic power from below, won land and other victories, and developed forms of life such as autonomous communes, food gardens, crèches, and political schools.

Crucially, the history recounts the tremendous cost of this struggle, including unrelenting repression, violence, betrayal, and the assassination of numerous comrades and leaders, which continually tested the movement's commitment to dignity, ethical discipline, and principled conduct.

We Are Still Not Counted as Human

On 21 March 2005 you gave a speech in the hall in the Kennedy Road shack settlement in Durban. More than a thousand people had just been beaten back from the local police station with rubber bullets and stun grenades after demanding that 14 people arrested on a road blockade two days earlier be released. Their demand was "Release them or arrest us all. If they are criminal then we are all criminal." In that speech you said "We are now alone." Can you take us back to that moment?

That was the moment when we realised that freedom and the African National Congress (ANC) were two different things. We had been promised a small piece of land near to the settlement for housing. Suddenly, without explanation, the land was being worked on, there was a grader and the people working there told us that it had been bought by a businessman who was going to build a brick factory.

We blocked the road to demand that the councillor come and meet with us to explain what was going on. We wanted to talk but they sent the police to beat us. When the councillor finally arrived in an armoured police vehicle he said that we were criminals and that we must be arrested.

That was the greatest disappointment. It was not just a disappointment that they lied about the land. It was also that they couldn't even come and explain what had changed. It was clear that we were outside of this democracy, and that our demand to be included in discussions about our own lives was being treated as criminal. It was clear that others would think and decide for us, that we did not count.

Two of the 14 people who were arrested were not adults and yet they were taken to an adult prison. They were all taken as dangerous criminals and denied bail. It was another shock.

When we marched on the police station it was Human Rights Day. The 14 people who had been arrested on the blockade had been charged with public violence even though the only violence that day came from the police. Violence from the police was not taken as violence but our demand to be recognised as part of the public was taken as violence. That's when we actually realised that we are not part of the public, we are just nonsense in the city. It was very clear that the public referred to the middle class people and the rich.

On 30 March the 14 people arrested on the road blockade were released. When they were welcomed back to Kennedy Road you gave another speech. You said that "The first Nelson Mandela was Jesus Christ. The second was Nelson Rolihlahla Mandela. The third Nelson Mandela are the poor people of the world." Where were you when Mandela was released? What did it mean to you?

I was in school. I was 14. We were divided at that time. It was the time of the war between Inkatha and the UDF [United Democratic Front]. People could easily draw the line between the two sides along a river or a road. Everyone on one side was Inkatha, everyone on the other side was UDF. A lot of people were killed or had their homes burnt down just because they were living on this or that side of the line between the two sides. I found myself on the Inkatha side.

I was forced into the war. At that time young men on both sides were forced into the war. If you refused you would be identified as a traitor, it was assumed that you must be on the other side. If you were identified as a traitor your family's house would be burnt. There was no way to say that you were just against the killing.

There was war in broad daylight. People had guns but we as young people, we did not have guns, we had sticks. If you turned back you would be shot. You had to face bullets from the front and the back. Somebody was shot right next to me. I stayed with him, to look after him, to drag him back to an ambulance. This allowed me to avoid the killing. He died in hospital. Other boys died that day too. Terrible things happened, very painful things. We don't talk about it.

When the news came that Mandela would be released there was huge excitement, huge celebration among some people. For some people it was the opening of the world. But for others the world was shutting down. I remember a young man, a real believer in Inkatha, who said that he would kill himself if Mandela became president. He passed over soon after the election.

What did all the talk of freedom mean for you?

I was very young but thinking of freedom at that time it was really about peace. It was about the end of war, the end of the politic of blood.

And for your hopes for your own life?

Well, I was still schooling. A lot of families around me had unemployed people so they worked the land. Others worked away from home, doing domestic work, working on farms, or in the cities. It was not just the people who were poor. The schools were also poor. That in itself is a lesson to children, a lesson that they do not matter. It was hard for us to see a life for ourselves outside of what we knew. There was no graduate for us to look up to. We had no guidance on what we could do after school. But somehow I wanted to go to university and become a lawyer.

Did you have any sense that studying law could be a path into a social project?

Well, my mother raised my two sisters my brother and I on her own. My father was not working. He was not able to pay inhlawulo. Marriage was a privilege. She had to leave us when she went to work for a white family in Estcourt. That was troubling me. You cry when your mother is leaving you without understanding that she's going to work for you, that she goes because she wants to take care of you. You ask yourself if it's really normal for a mother to leave her children, you ask yourself why this is happening. As a child you don't understand the history that has made some people poor and other people rich. You don't understand the system that keeps some people poor and others rich. All you know is that your mother is leaving you. At most she could come back once a month, but not every month.

My mother didn't have a home of her own. We didn't have a home. We lived with different families when she left. That was the thing

3

most troubling me. So we lived with different families, some related, some not related, in different villages, including Emmaus in Bergville which is where my father's parents were. I went to four different primary schools. I was able to stay in one high school for all five years though, Bonokuhle High School in eMangweni in Estcourt which is my mother's side.

We were always changing families and changing schools. For me that is deep, because some of the families were so poor too, and they were finding it difficult to afford to care for their own children, but they welcome us as their children. Sometimes my mother would not be able to support them or support us. She would just leave us with them. But they gave me their love. That was unbelievable. Sometimes I feel like I owe them now that I have grown up. Just thanking them was not enough.

I still feel haunted by this but I also feel gratitude to all the people, poor people, who opened their homes and families to me. I grew up with many different families and was shaped by these different families. I tasted different ways of living with different families.

The white family that my mother worked for were kind to her, and they were kind to us, her children, when we visited over a weekend or for a week during the school holidays. When I got there, the kids would be happy, they would welcome me. They did not see me as a strange person. They were really happy to see me. We would play. Their sons would lend me their bikes and I learned to ride. When you are sharing this joy you feel the same. But even as a young child you start to ask why your mother must leave you to look after other children, why one family has a nice house and another has no home, why one family can remain together and another is torn apart, why some children have bikes and toys and others have nothing but what they can make for themselves. So for me freedom meant that every family should be able to have a good home, the same comfort, that every family should be able to be together if they wanted to.

But my hope of being able to go to the university, to become a lawyer, was more of a moral obligation rather than something to do with politics. As a child from a very poor family, a child with no real home, a child sent to poor schools, a child expected to go and kill other poor children, well, the Boy Scouts was one place outside of the families that cared for me where I was welcomed and taken serious. There we talked a lot about making the world a better place, about leaving it better than you found it, about life as a kind of moral test. So for me when Mandela was released and the world was opening freedom was pretty much around the moral sense, the sense that the humanity of everyone should be recognised, that everyone should be given the same care and respect.

You finished school in 1996, two years after Mandela became president. That was still a time of real optimism for many people.

Yes, I felt the world was changing. I was so excited when I got a letter of acceptance from the university. I thought it was that simple: you apply, you get accepted.

But then I had to face the real world. I must travel to Durban. I needed a place to stay, food, books. Most of all I needed to pay the university fees. It really stressed me. I felt really alone. My brother-in-law offered me a place to stay though. When I took the bus to the university we would pass Kennedy Road, this huge shack settlement on a hill below a rubbish dump.

I couldn't find the money for the fees and then my brother-in-law moved to Johannesburg.

It all just got cut. This happened to many black people. People at home had hopes in me but I saw myself as a failure. I was thinking more and more about committing suicide. You are no longer a child. You are now a man. You are on your own.

It was at this stage that I felt oppression. I felt that I was on the wrong terrain, that I was not fit to be a student. I asked myself why I thought in the first place that I could go to university, that I should have known from the onset that it's not for somebody like me.

Kennedy Road was the way out for me. Accepting that I had been defeated, giving up on my hope of going to the university and moving to Kennedy Road liberated me from the extreme stress that I was suffering.

After a while I found a job at a petrol station, a job as a petrol attendant. It was close, I could walk to work. After a couple of years I was promoted. Life was moving forward.

And how was life in Kennedy Road?

Well growing up I thought that I knew what it was to be poor but when I got to Kennedy Road I came to realise that I was not as poor as I thought I was. In that way setting my feet in Kennedy Road was devastating. But people were welcoming.

When a normal person sees children eating the worms at the toilet, a child being bitten on the head by a rat, a baby burnt in a fire or people being so badly treated by the police they want to do something about it. But at first I thought, like lots of people do, that the people in the settlement were not doing enough, that they were either ignorant or not interested. There was kind of a blaming. I blamed people living there. I thought they were not doing enough about those conditions. I was still optimistic about the ANC and I thought people didn't know how to engage with them, that they didn't know how changes comes about. So I got involved in the ANC and was elected as the deputy chairperson of the ward.

But going to the ANC meetings at night really discouraged me. At the ward level the meetings were dominated by middle class people, people living in big houses. Meetings could finish at 11 or 12 at night and none of the middle class people thought to offer us lifts back to the shacks in their cars. I was carrying a mandate from the people who had elected me in Kennedy Road but there was no interest in that. At the time the ANC was not so much about tenders. It was about positions and power; who do we put in power, who to mobilise against, who to support when conferences were coming up. Often we did not know the people we were meant to support or oppose. I could not live through that for a very long time.

In 2004 there was a big meeting about a proposed housing development in Kennedy Road with various government departments. It was a deciding moment. We were not invited and we were never told the outcome of the meeting. Eventually we came to know that the meeting opposed the housing development. They didn't want us to live with middle class people. They wanted to take us to human dumping grounds far outside the city, even further out than the townships built under apartheid.

I left the ANC in 2004 and at the same time the Kennedy Road Development Committee declared 2005 as the year of action.

That's interesting because 2004 is the year that people across the country, mostly people living in shacks, started organising road blockades. That's the year in which what some people called the rebellion of the poor began.

Yes, I remember when Tebogo Mkhonza was killed by the police in a protest in the Free State. He was 17. We saw the protests through the media but we had no connection to what was happening. What caught my mind was the fact that when you see people blockading roads on the television and you read about it in the newspaper you realise that people are doing the same thing in different places without knowing each other or speaking to each other.

After we organised the road blockade on 19 March we began to meet with other nearby settlements and a number of protests were organised from different settlements against local councillors. On 4 October at a meeting of leaders from 14 settlements we decided to form one organisation, Abahlali baseMjondolo. Our demands for land and housing in the city were clear, and at least understood even if opposed. But we also insisted that we must be recognised as people who, like all other people, think, as people who should be included in discussions and decision making, as people who should not be treated like children or criminals, as people whose dignity should be respected. This demand was not understood.

It was taken as noise rather than speech.

Yes.

The emphasis on being recognised as people who think came through those early meetings very clearly. But there were two other concepts, your concepts, that were developed as ideas to guide the new politics that was being worked out: the need for 'a politics of the poor' and 'living politics'. Can you explain their significance?

Well, when we found that trying to engage the state was taken as criminal it was clear that the forms of politics that existed at that time excluded the poor. Neither the national government nor any of the city councils wanted to collaborate with the poor to resolve the problems of the poor. No political party represented the poor, and the trade unions represented their members, not the millions of poor people outside of formal employment.

We needed our own politics, a politics that would be by and for the poor, a politics that would be a space for the poor to think together, build our power together and express and advance our interests.

At the time it was not thought that the poor deserved dignity. All kinds of other people thought that they should think for us, decide for us. Development that was said to be for us was not with us, and it was often against our interests. Sometimes it made us poorer by destroying our homes and dumping us far outside of the cities in houses that were worse than our shacks.

So the politics of the poor meant that we would develop our own language, our own ideas - that we wouldn't have to speak their language and rely on their ideas. We needed a politics that didn't just mean that the poor must mindlessly obey the politicians, the government officials and the NGOs.

It was at this time that we adopted the slogan 'nothing for us, without us'. We did not develop it but it expressed what we felt. We still do not want politicians to 'deliver' to us or to govern for us. They should govern with us. All development should be participatory.

We needed a politics that would make sense to the masses of this country. For this the thinking that is always already there in shack settlements and rural villages, the places where poor communities live, needed to be organised, focused and connected.

We were kind of living two lives. There was the life where the well-off were telling us that we must learn their language to be accepted, that anyone who didn't know that language was ignorant and there was the life of the people with the language of the people. We had to organise our thinking and our power to be able to take the issues and hopes of the poor into that what is called the mainstream even though it is the world of a minority. We were the majority and I thought a new politics - new narrative, a new language, a living politics, a living communism was necessary.

We understood and still understand a living politics to be a politics that can be understood by everyone, whether old or young, no matter how good a person is at English or how many years of schooling they have had. A politics that is not of and by the people is useless. A politics that is not understood, owned and directed by the people is useless. In fact it becomes just another form of exclusion and oppression even if it says it is for the people.

There is nothing that cannot be explained to the people, nothing that cannot be translated into their language. If you speak in a way that means that you cannot be understood that is a choice, and it is a choice to try and raise yourself above the people, to feel that you are superior to them, to exclude them.

At the time when you raised the idea of 'a living communism' you did so in the tone of a question rather than an answer. You said, speaking in a way that reaches into the unknown, that 'we need something like a living communism.'

Well a living communism would have to be a living politics. It would need to have space for the politics of the poor, along with other kinds of politics. For me communism needed to be grounded in community. My understanding was that in order to be able to liberate ourselves from oppression we would need a political praxis grounded in community praxis and that we would first need to build communities. We needed a different way of being in community and a way to embrace the ability of a community to be able to liberate itself as a community. We needed to build communities of communities.

Today we speak about building a movement of communes and a movement of movements so the idea of community remains at the heart of everything. You don't just suddenly become a community because you happen to have homes, houses, close together. That does not automatically make communities. Communities are built. We wanted to build communities and join them into a force that could challenge the systems of oppression.

The response from the ANC and the local state, and some other actors, to the emergence of a movement, a movement outside of their control was intensely hostile.

Yes, there was constant police harassment. The police physically prevented us from participating in public discussions on radio and television. I and another comrade were stopped by the police while travelling to a radio station, arrested and tortured. Our organisation was treated as a conspiracy, a criminal conspiracy. It was constantly said that we were criminals being remoted by a white man working for a foreign government, as if we couldn't think and speak for ourselves.

You have spoken about how that night in the holding cells, after being tortured in the police station was a personal turning point.

While I was being beaten by Nayager [Glen Nayager, the head of the local police station], while my head was being banged on the wall, I was constantly asked who the hell do I think I am to think I can lead ignorant people, rubbish people, to think that we have a right to live with middle class people, to be part of society. He also asked me if I think I am a Jesus Christ that can liberate all those jondolos [shack dwellers].

10

When you are being beaten the physical pain, the physical damage, is one thing. But there was also an emotional assault. The inner pain, the inner damage, I found it very stressful. Why is there so much hatred when all you are asking is for the dignity of everyone to be respected, for us all to be human beings among other human beings? It may be difficult to heal that one because it leads to depression. You go off, you go mad.

Having to live with this double headache, the physical headache of having been banged on the bricks of the walls of the office, and the emotional headache I was dealing with, made me to have to think throughout the night. There was no sleep. And it was my first time being arrested, being in holding cells. I asked myself 'who the hell am I?'. I asked myself who was ordering the police to do this. I asked myself if I should continue with the struggle.

Then comes the dawn without me having had any sleep. I'm on my own, separated from the people who have asked me to lead, who have given me that responsibility, and Nayager vandalised that. He places me in a dehumanised kind of a moment where I see myself as worthless, infected, a disaster and a disgrace. I was reduced to weightlessness. That's how he reduced me.

But then when I came to the court I heard that there were so many people in red shirts outside the court, in the corridors of the court. When I came up the stairs into the dock in the court there were so many. Everyone was quiet, nobody could speak, but I felt the power of all the people there. I took the decision to commit my life to this struggle.

When people talk about solidarity it always comes to my mind that solidarity must be at a personal level. You need to know that people are saying that you are not alone. People can collapse when they are alone. You see the end of everything. It causes irreparable damage if people ever feel alone.

The repression continued.

Yes, it got worse in 2006 when there was an election and we followed the position of the LPM [Landless People's Movement] who had said 'No Land! No Vote!' in the 2004 election.

They were repressed and some of their people were tortured. We said 'No Land! No House!

No Vote!'. We had now connected with the LPM in Johannesburg and the Western Cape Anti-Eviction Campaign in Cape Town and no longer felt alone. We took a combined movement position. This wasn't just taken as criminal. It was taken as treason.

This is when I lost my job. My boss started bullying me. He would call me in and show me newspaper articles about our movement and the campaign. One day I saw him having coffee with Mike Sutcliffe [the ANC City Manager at the time]. I was then told that I was being given leave to go and tell people to vote. It was said on the radio that I had told people to go and vote. I explained on the radio that this was not true and that people themselves had decided not to vote. That is how I lost my job. Other people also lost their jobs in these early years. I became more conscious of how oppression works. Before then I had thought that politics and business were two different things.

Late on the night before the election the ANC wanted to open the City Hall to negotiate with us. We were starting to understand our power as the organised poor, the strong poor.

In 2007 we organised a collective march on the Mayor, a combined action by all the branches in the different settlements. We carefully followed all the legal requirements but the march was banned. When it was decided to march in defiance of the ban – which was illegal – we were attacked with batons, stun grenades, rubber bullets and live ammunition. Our march had been peaceful but the world was told that we were violent. We were shown as criminals.

We were treated as if we were beneath their law, as if we were not worthy of being human.

Refusing to vote was taken as treason, and met with violence, but trying to exercise the democratic right to peaceful protest was also met with violence and criminalisation.

Yes, it became clear that poor people must be good boys and girls and support other people to speak for them, whether politicians, NGOs or academics, but that we must not think and speak for ourselves. We began to reflect on who we were at the time. It was clear that being poor and black meant that you did not matter to society, that you were not counted as human. And if you lived in the shacks in the middle class suburbs your mere existence, your mere presence, was taken as criminal. When we were not allowed to march on the mayor it was not just the ANC that was keeping us out of democracy, the rest of society was quiet. We knew that there were structures in society to support democracy, that there were other communities, but what was done to us was accepted. We started hearing middle class people saying that we were devaluing their homes, that we were criminals. It became clear that democracy was not what we had thought. It was clear that there was a class question. It was clear that we were not only not wanted by the state, but by the society as a whole. As this became clearer the movement grew.

When the state beat and arrested us when we tried to participate in democracy they thought that they were giving us a lesson to know our place, to stay in our dark corners. They didn't realise that they were giving a different lesson to poor people, a lesson that this democracy was not for us and that we had to organise to be strong together.

This repression continued for some years.

In 2006 the movement sent another electric shock into the political order when it decided to hold UnFreedom Day [on the national holiday Freedom Day that celebrates the end of apartheid].

Yes, it came out of a series of meetings in our movement and with other organisations. UnFreedom Day came as a result of deep discussions about the meaning of freedom. People were clear that we could not accept to be bussed into the stadiums to listen to politicians tell us that we were free when we were being kicked out of democracy, forced out of our homes at gunpoint. People were clear that there cannot be freedom without land, without housing, without access to basic services, without being taken as people who have the same right as all other people to participate in discussions and decision making. It has been an annual event since then.

In 2006 we had started holding UnFreedom Day events on Freedom Day. The City and the police tried to shut it down. In 2009 we held the event inside the Kennedy Road settlement, far from any roads and middle class houses. They even tried to shut that down. When we went ahead they had a police helicopter flying just above the meeting.

The event itself is not as important as the debates and the discussion among people around what freedom means to them. We'll have those discussions leading to the event and so the event becomes a yardstick to measure the thinking of the people.

But we kept going despite the repression and although there were many arrests, a number of leaders lost their jobs and many people were injured our persistence eventually ensured that we won the right to organise marches, participate in debates on radio and TV, and so on. Today these rights are no longer contested.

To get here we also had to assert our autonomy from the NGOs. We were still thinking that the ANC and the state are troublesome but that society is innocent. The lesson we learnt from our experience with the NGOs was that the system of oppression is much bigger than just the ANC and state. We realised that there were people, self-appointed people, who thought they had the responsibility to think for the poor, to direct our struggles and to decide on our future. They would bus poor people into meetings without us having any say about the agenda. They wanted to think for us, not with us. It was quite disappointing because we thought learned people, academics and NGO bosses, had enough education to know that they should support people to emancipate themselves, not to appoint themselves as the vanguard of revolution, not to think for us and direct us. When we, together with the LPM and the Anti-Eviction Campaign, boycotted the Social Movements Indaba, the big NGO meeting, at the end of 2006 and decided to build our own movement platform they attacked us in the media, they called us criminals. They have never stopped hating us for the crime of taking our dignity seriously.

The insistence on dignity has always been central to your struggle, and it appears in the struggles of impoverished people around the country, around the world too.

When we started our struggle the view that all that we could struggle for was 'service delivery' was very dominant. Our struggle was also said to be a 'service delivery' struggle. Of course we needed basic services, everyone needs water, sanitation and electricity. But for us the recognition of our humanity, of our dignity, was the most important thing. For us, the question of dignity is that you respect us, and how do you respect us? You engage with us in a respectful way, you allow us to speak what we think is right. We wanted to engage, we wanted to fully participate in decision making. We didn't want people to 'deliver' services to us. We wanted to participate in development. We wanted the state and the NGOs to think with us, not for us. That actually sealed the significance of dignity in our politics.

We came to realise that actually why people lie to us, why they make fake promises to us, is because in their eyes we are not human enough. It is very deep. It is very painful. If someone wants to think for you, speak for you and do things for you, well, that renders you useless. A human being deserves dignity, something that you are born with.

An eviction case is not just an eviction case. It is about human beings. All this technical talk of wanting to lay statistics over people takes away the responsibility that we owe to each other as human beings.

A person is not taken seriously when their humanity is not recognised. People with power see no reason to account to objects, because that's basically what dehumanisation means. We are taken as objects, as objects or as a kind of animal. If you are not even allowed to think then all the opportunities of life, of being human with other human beings, are banned for you. It takes away the essence of having a mind, of being human. This is why we always said that our humanity, our dignity, is not negotiable. Many things can be negotiated but not this.

If 2004 was the year in which protests by impoverished people began to challenge the elite nationalism of the ANC, 2008 was the year in which impoverished people, often encouraged by local elites, turned on other. You had been warning, for years, that 'the anger of the poor can go in many directions.'

Yes, when migrants were attacked and killed in broad daylight it presented us with a moment of self, of introspection. We needed to reflect on the things we say, on the commitment we make and the contribution we make in society.

It can happen that when oppressed people feel disrespected they try to regain some sense of respect by turning on other oppressed people, by trying to make themselves feel better than other people. We had been talking about dignity for ourselves but in 2008 we had to affirm that we mean dignity for everyone. We said that a person is a person wherever they may find themselves, no matter where they were born.

That moment presented us with an opportunity, again, to be tested on what we commit to, and it broadened our strategy and our under-standing of freedom. Is it enough that I am free? What about others? What about my neighbours? There is no real freedom without others being free, without your neighbours being free. This tells a story about the human consciousness in relation to others.

We were able to affirm that the struggle we were engaged in was a sacrifice, a good place to talk about real freedom, freedom that does not limit or confine itself to a particular goal. We saw a bigger picture of humanity, which represents the universal definition of what a human being can be.

Of course we also saw that xenophobia, and then ethnicity too, is intentionally used to divide poor people, people who feel themselves to be the same, when they pose a danger to the system. So, from time to time, the system has to shape them, has to remind them that they are not the same, and that they must see each other as enemies. That is by design. The system must make poor people think that they are denying each other's opportunities to a flourishing life. We must be divided by language, gender, sexuality. This hate will keep us all poor. Because this hate always weakens the poor it has to be rejected by poor people first. We have to continue to build our consciousness, to connect with struggles around the world, to learn from each other.

When you take a principled position numbers don't matter. Anyone is important. In fact, every individual makes us all. The question of minority versus majority doesn't work in the definition of a human being. You don't have to be a majority to be a human being.

Abahlali takes a very clear line on these questions.

Soon after the ANC conceded your right to participate in the formal political sphere it shifted repression towards informal violence, violence backed by the police but not carried out by the police.

Yes, we were attacked in the Kennedy Road settlement on the 26th and 27th of September 2009. We were having a youth camp at the hall in Kennedy Road. We also had a concert in the community hall, and there was a soccer tournament at the sports ground. A lot was happening on the 26th.

These guys who attacked us knew that I was going to be at the camp but that afternoon I had to leave to Estcourt to be with my mother. It was unplanned. If I was there I am sure that one of two things would happen. Either I would have been killed, I would have offered my own life, or I would have been able to stop the violence meaning that the two lives that were lost that night would not have been lost. Our leaders and people from the Eastern Cape were attacked, homes were ransacked and set alight. And then people were arrested, only people from the Eastern Cape.

The attack continued during the broad daylight in front of the police. The police, the metro police, the public order police, intelligence. They were all there. But people's homes were still set alight. The violence continued.

That day very senior ANC politicians, ministers, came to Kennedy Road and launched a propaganda. They said that we were 'running our own authority', that Abahlali was responsible for violence, and for the lives that were lost, and that 'Abahlali has been disbanded'. They went to parliament and said that 'Kennedy Road has been liberated'. Senior ANC people were saying these things, people like Willies Mchunu. That means that attack was planned at a very high political level.

People are killed in the shacks every weekend. Senior police officers do not come. You never see a politician. Our lives count for nothing. Suddenly they were all there. Even Nayager said that this was planned at a high level. He said he had done his work for almost forty years and there was nothing special about the killing of poor black people and now all these politicians are there. He even came to our offices in Durban and made an apology. He confessed that he was under political pressure when he repressed us. I think he was regretting. He had a very guilty conscience. He was prepared to testify. And then of course he died.

For us it was now clear that the ANC was no longer to be trusted. They had actually turned themselves into an enemy of the people. We no longer had a government that we could trust.

Even our lawyer was very scared, she felt scared to represent us. It's an experience that one would never forget.

After apartheid, political violence has mostly been police killings and assassinations but this was like the 1980s. Men were mobilised, armed and given alcohol. There was a strong ethnic dimension. Abahlali was said to be an Mpondo organisation.

Yes there was a clear and direct connection to that because, you know, that was really a war. I was in Estcourt and people were phoning me.

I could hear that this was war. My family had to flee and hide. It was like the 80s. You know, when you run, you do not know where to hide, who's going to get hurt. And these ANC guys saying that Kennedy Road was for Zulus, that I was imposing Mpondo people on them. Our movement had united people. We did not see each other as Zulus or Xhosas. This unity was presented as a kind of treason.

Of course at the time Zuma had incited this whole ethnic politics, this Zulu politics. He campaigned by saying that the Zulu people were occupied by the Xhosa people. He used ethnic politics to find his way to power and it worked for him. It became the politics of the day. It created damage and division in the community. They made their ethnic politics very clear when only Xhosa-speaking people were arrested.

Our offices were destroyed. Our library was destroyed. We had to go underground. We were scattered all over the place. At first we met secretly in a funeral parlour. Then we started meeting openly in a park.

And then, in 2013, the assassinations started.

Yes, they assassinated Nkululeko Gwala, a leader in our movement in Cato Crest, on 26 June 2013. The ANC had openly threatened him. Sibongiseni Dhlomo, who is now a Deputy Cabinet minister, made a public threat against Nkululeko on the day he was murdered.

We had survived the attack in Kennedy Road. We had eventually been vindicated in court. Now they started to use assassinations. The ANC was sending a very clear message to us that we had no right to organise ourselves, no right to organise without their authority. They were saying that we were liberated by uMkhonto weSizwe, by the ANC, and that this gives them a legitimate right to rule, to steal and to defend their rule and their stealing with violence.

They spoke as if the people had done nothing to liberate themselves. As if there was not a mass struggle. As if the Black Consciousness movement, the UDF and Cosatu did not exist. The people are not seen in the history told by the ANC and they are repressed if they want to be part of the present.

You gave an electric speech at Nkululeko's funeral. It was on the front page of Isolezwe. It was on uKhozi FM. It was a real moment because they were trying to terrify people into submission and you confronted them at the funeral.

The funeral was incredibly tense. It was held at Nkululeko's home village in Inchanga. And, you know, hearing that someone was shot there is a feeling that the inclusion of people involved in a struggle with that person must be people of violence. The ANC tried to make it an ANC funeral. That's how dangerous they can be. They can actually kill you and then offer to bury you, to pay for the funeral.

James Nxumalo, who was the mayor at that time, was present. He also came from this village. There were other high profile government people, lots of police, intelligence. The local ANC councillor spoke first, setting the tone. He was implying that this was an ANC funeral, that this village is an ANC home. Nkululeko's father was a loyal ANC member so he was moving to capture the family first. He went on to say that this is an ANC ward and that the ANC is conducting this funeral. He said that there are no shacks in the village but that people from the shacks are here. He was mocking our poverty. When he was setting the ground, he was creating threats, making it difficult for any other speaker who is non-ANC.

The warning was very clear. We felt really threatened.

After he spoke, the senior leaders of the movement took me to the side and they counselled me not to speak. They warned me that it was too dangerous. But then the master of ceremonies, appointed by the family, called me to speak. Our members from Cato Crest had come in buses. Nkululeko was loved by the community. There were red shirts everywhere. We could not show fear. And anyway I was fuming, not scared, just really angry at the situation, at the lies and hypocrisy.

I spoke very diplomatically, saying, very respectfully, that the family needed and deserved to know the truth. I deliberately went against every single thing that the councillor had said. I explained how we knew Nkululeko, how we understood him, what he meant to the community and the movement. I explained that people in rural communities like this village had been abandoned, just like poor people in the cities, and that Nkululeko had given his life for the people, for the oppressed.

I pointed out how many Abahlali members were there to honour their leader, and that nobody would tell us what to say and what not to say, that in fact we were there to tell the truth about how he was killed. I explained that Nkululeko was killed for his bravery and honesty. I made it clear that senior ANC politicians had publicly threatened him and now there were ANC politicians at the funeral wanting to make it an ANC funeral. Emotions were very high. People were moaning. The marquee was shaking. The police stood up, the intelligence. After my speech, the ANC people, including the mayor, could not proceed to speak. The councillor disappeared. It was clear that the ANC were unwelcome. Immediately after the speech my comrades pulled me out, put me in a car. They felt I was in danger, that it would not be safe to proceed to the grave. But the members stayed and it became an Abahlali funeral.

When you have to speak for people, you have to do justice to the people. You to make sure that you say everything that they would have said. It is not about you. I had to satisfy them without fear for myself. After I spoke I was at peace, having said what I needed to say and confident that I had represented the emotions of our members.

There were also two police killings in Cato Crest in that same year. A police officer was convicted for one of the killings.

Yes. Nkosinathi Mngomezulu was shot by the police, shot a number of times, and seriously wounded during an eviction on 22 September. He really suffered. He had to carry a bag for his urine. It took several months for him to die, getting weaker and weaker every day. At the end he was helpless.

Nqobile Nzuza was killed by the police during a protest against evictions on 30 September. She was 17. A senior ANC politician offered the Nzuza family taxis and other support for Nqobile's funeral.

These evictions were illegal. We had a court order preventing evictions. But the ANC assume that they are above the law and that we are below the law. They just ignored the court order. We are always criminals, even when the law is on our side. The ANC take the lives of poor black people as if they count for nothing. It's like we are just rubbish, not human beings. The ANC has reduced the humanity of people to the extent where it is normal to vandalise humanity. It's very scary.

When Nqobile was killed the police said that they were under attack by a vicious mob and had to shoot to save their lives. They spoke as if they were the real victims. The media repeated this as if it were true. They saw no reason to talk to eyewitnesses, to people who were part of the protest. We were made to look like savages.

This continues to happen. When Zamekile Shangase was murdered by the police in Lamontville on 29 July 2021 during a 'show your receipt' raid [a police raid in which food and other items are confiscated if people cannot show a purchase receipt] the police said that they fired in self-defence because they were coming under fire from all sides. The media repeated this as if it were fact, as did some academics and political commentators.

Nobody fired on the police at any time.

Although Nkosinathi was killed with live ammunition during an illegal eviction the police officer was found not guilty. This is usually how things go. But when the matter of Nqobile's killing finally went to court after five years a police officer was convicted and we were vindicated. It was shown that Nqobile was unarmed and shot from behind, that there was no mob attack on the police.

And then they assassinated Thuli Ndlovu in 2014, S'bonelo Mpeku in 2017, S'fiso Ngcobo in 2018. There were others too. In 2016 two ANC councillors were convicted of the murder of Thuli Ndlovu. This seemed to be a turning point in getting the media, human rights organisations and so on to understand what was happening.

Yes. Poor black people are just not believed when we talk about the repression we face unless the courts, or middle class people like journalists, filmmakers or academics confirm the truth of what we are saying, and even then these people can come under real pressure.

This is part of how oppression works.

There is such a high level of brutality, such a low level of consciousness. Thuli was shot with a baby on her back, a young woman carrying a baby, a young woman who actually caused no threats to anyone. She was a mother of two.

When the two ANC councillors were convicted it did help to show that it was the ANC that was killing us. But the ANC have never come to mourn, never come to apologise. Even Zandile Gumede [the former Durban mayor, now being criminally prosecuted for corruption] having heard that Thuli had a daughter who was just finishing matric at the time, never even considered to make sure that her daughter, Sli, was able to pursue a university degree. We are proud that the movement supported her. She is now a qualified teacher.

It is not just us who are being assassinated. There is also Fikile Ntshangase, Babita Deokaran. So many. So many people are also killed on protests. The killing continues. You cannot see any effort to end the killing. They have so much money but they don't use it to bring healthy minds together to discuss how to stop the killing, to research internationally to see how other countries have dealt with this. All this killing is not seen as a crisis. The defiling of humanity has become normalised.

The ANC should be using the power of the people to confront the colonial system that continues to terrorise us and vandalise our humanity but instead they are using violence to repress the people so that they can benefit from the system.

The police kill more people here than in the US but here is no mass movement against police violence here. It seems as if our society as a whole has a high tolerance for state violence.

There should be a public outcry when even one life is taken. But poor black people do not count to this society. This is a problem throughout society. You see it very clearly in the media.

The movements that emerged at the turn of the century collapsed for a number of reasons. In some cases repression was a key factor. It often led to paranoia, division, a general breakdown in trust and a centralisation of authority. How has Abahlali come through this horrific level of repression, with more than twenty lives having been lost? With more than 120 000 members in 87 branches the movement is larger than it has ever been and it has sustained democratic organising at this significantly increased scale.

I think it's the question of dignity in life, a question of humanity. We started with this and kept dignity at the centre. The movement is grounded in the principles and values of ubuntu. That's where we built our foundation. We did not allow people to define us as just being about service delivery or anything else that reduces the meaning and value of the movement. We centred our humanity.

A lot of people think, can only think, that we can only come together because of our living conditions. Of course that is important, and we struggle very hard to improve those conditions. But when we are together, the first thing is to recognise each and everyone's humanity, because it's only from that position of humanity that we come together to take our place as people amongst other people on this earth. We come together because our humanity is troubled. We come together to develop and defend our humanity, to make the world more human, more in keeping with the dignity of human being. It is after this that questions of living conditions and service delivery then come into being. The fact that we are not just about service delivery has actually helped us sustain the movement during very hard times.

Of course there are people in the movement who have been offered houses by the government with an intent to shut their mouths. This is a test to see if we are really just about houses and services. We have passed that test. The question of our humanity is far bigger than just service delivery.

The camps [all night meetings] are central because we don't just talk about material issues.

We also talk about the systems of care that make us more human.

And the movement came to socialism, and then to this vision of building socialism from below from communes, through humanism. Humanism remains the measure of politics as well as its foundation.

Ubuntu as a way to define how each human being should behave in relation to others becomes an idea that goes beyond the village, it goes into broader society, into broader questions of how we relate to each other. It is a broader political spirit of humanism that also appeals to the questions of freedom and liberation.

Socialism, democratic socialism built from below, democratic socialism in the hands of the people, is the political form to humanise society. Lindokuhle [Lindokuhle Mnguni, a young leader in the movement assassinated in 2022] always said that socialism has to be something you live together, something you practice together. When I talk about Ubuntu, it is not just a concept I'm referring to, not just an idea, but the praxis that demonstrates our humanity, that builds our humanity, that defends our humanity.

In 2018 you had to go underground again.

When you know that a decision has been taken to have you killed there is a lot on your mind. You have to consider a lot. I had to recognise and remember that it was not about me and that I had the responsibility to protect people around me. I had a responsibility to protect my family and other leaders, other young leaders.

Going underground, underground on your own, creates a big problem of self-isolation. Sometimes it seems like a bigger problem than the problem that forced you underground. When you have a story that is only known by you it is terrible. The need to go underground to stay alive, to keep people around you safe, captured me and put me into a different planet, a planet of my own. Psychologically and spiritually I was removed from the earth. had a lot to think about. I had to think about all the things that I had not achieved in life, knowing that I could be killed at any time but also knowing that I did not have much option to avoid this. I thought a lot about what would become of my children. The nights were sleepless. I felt that I had been buried alive. There was fear, not fear of death itself, but fear of what my death would mean for the people that were connected to me.

I think that was the most difficult moment. But ultimately the whole thing reminded me that the point of creating fear, of those threats, was not just to remove me from the movement, it was to remove me from society. And because a leader is shaped and sustained by the people that choose them to lead it was a way to remove the influence of those people from society, to destroy their power. In a way it is a kind of spiritual war too, a war to destroy the idea that every human being counts, that every human being deserves dignity.

You were underground from May to December, but in September, with the movement facing a serious crisis, you emerged at that month's General Assembly. It was an extraordinary moment. And then the following month there was the massive protest against repression, after which the tide turned and it became possible for you to come back into a more ordinary although still heavily secured life.

It was a serious crisis. We had some people who had some standing in the movement because they had suffered in 2009, as a result of the attack. Without any democratic process they sent the women's choir to perform at a campaign event for Nkosazana Dlamini-Zuma [who was running for the presidency of the ANC at that time] at the ICC [International Convention Centre]. They felt very angry and humiliated when they realised that they were at an ANC event.

When the choir came back there was huge anger in the movement.

26

It became clear that a small group of people had been captured by the ANC. They had been offered money and business opportunities through VBS Bank, the bank that was looted by the politicians, and through the undertakers' association that was aligned to Jacob Zuma.

The whole leadership was recalled pending a new election via a motion from the floor at the General Assembly. The right to recall is essential for any democratic organisation and it saved the movement. The problem was resolved by the members but it was felt that I had to be there to give the members confidence that repression had not defeated us. The march against repression early in October was huge, and I appeared there too. The members won the space for me to return, and for some time the assassinations stopped.

The people who were captured by the ANC recently returned and apologised. There has been healing.

The emergence of Lindokuhle as an extraordinary young leader, and the development of the eKhenana Commune seemed to expand the political imagination of the movement, and develop its practices in new directions.

Lindo was a brilliant cadre, a brilliant young man. Lindo and Ayanda [Ngila] started from the acknowledgement that there are no jobs for young people. From there they acknowledged that the hands that feed you will always control you. They were clear about the political stomach, that unless the poor and the working class own the means of production, the status quo shall remain. You will remain a subject of those who are in authority.

The idea of a commune came out of that discussion to say that if we want total liberation, we must occupy and use the land. They did so well that they began to be able to support the movement with their surplus. The sound system we are using today was bought for the movement by the commune.

We were reminded what land means to African people, what land means in the spirit of liberation. Before colonialism, before industrialisation, people could live with just land. So it was amazing in this century to have young people thinking about that, to decide that they can live without bosses and build economic and political freedom from a commune. Producing food was just the beginning.

There was the communal kitchen where they ate together and made sure that nobody ever went hungry. They had the youth club, the poetry project, which was amazing, and of course the Frantz Fanon Political School. The Commune became a resource for the whole movement, an inspiration. There is now a Lindokuhle Mnguni occupation in Johannesburg that is working towards becoming a commune.

Lindo had so many more ideas. He was a Marxist, of course, a communist. He had been reading from high school, he kept reading in prison. Steve Biko, Malcolm X, Karl Marx, Paulo Freire. Frantz Fanon, of course. And he was an internationalist. The first seeds for the garden came from the MST in Brazil. They would travel to Swaziland to be in solidarity with the movement there. They hosted people from around the world. And he was so strongly committed to women's equality, to building women's power. He would not entertain reactionary positions in the name of culture. He called that feudalism.

Lindo was not the kind of communist that tells people that they must obey a vanguard now so that the revolution can come later. He was building socialism from below. He understood socialism as something to be practiced now, he understood that you need a place to practice socialism, you need land and a community. He was so courageous. He introduced the slogan 'Socialism or death' to the movement. He knew he would die. He gave his life for the people, for an idea. Three comrades gave their lives for the Commune.

In South Africa the price for land continues to be paid in blood.

The movement has been able to build power from below and it has won all kinds of victories. But repression makes it hard to sustain popular power, and although you can win land, force changes in policies and bring thousands of people into the streets you do not have enough power, enough people, to

contest the broad trajectory of the state which remains the same – a mixture of neoliberal policies and violent kleptocratic practices. There is considerable pressure from your members to enter electoral politics.

Well, any individual elected into power is highly likely to be co-opted, to be made to join the system. What we have seen with the ANC is that black people can join the system, and give it legitimacy for a few years before people see that it remains the same. It could be the same if poor people take a place in the system. The system is designed for that. So we have to think beyond that. We have to think bigger than that.

During apartheid we thought we were only oppressed because of colour, but now we have realised that it was not just about the colour. At that time we did not speak about the system. Now we understand the system. Elections change faces and hands. How do you emancipate people out of a system that is able to use people that were most trusted to continue to oppress us? The system is smart enough to have your brother or your sister betray you.

We have to think about how we put the people in power, not individuals. That's the question that we have to be battling with because any individual is likely to be co-opted, corrupted, and changed by the system. We cannot enter the system just to give it a few years of legitimacy. We have to be wary of the system.

People used to talk about the construction of a democratic system. Now they talk about the reconstruction of the system. We began our struggle looking for an opportunity to negotiate, to engage. The ANC was completely arrogant and shattered those possibilities. It is now clear that we need to talk about the destruction of the capitalist system so that there can be a real reconstruction of a new system, a new system that places the people – and the humanity and dignity of all people - at the centre, a new system with a new relation to the world, to the earth, and all its people.

We were able to get this right to vote and we were told that democracy and freedom had now arrived. It was presented as though after voting people would able to exercise their full potential to enjoy life, to have access to the things required to enjoy life, and to live in a state of respect and equality. But immediately after the people voted the ANC into power all the promises of a new democracy were betrayed.

From the onset democracy and freedom were meant for a certain group of people. Some people have made progress, some have become wealthy out of the misery of others, while the poor get poorer. There is a lot of disappointment. The worst thing has been the level of violence.

Violence has been unleashed to limit democratic rights to participate in discussions and decision making, to keep people in fear. The fact that so many of our members have been killed, and that activists in other struggles and organisations have been killed too, is clear evidence that the state has chosen to become the enemy of the people.

Why do you think impoverished people have been violently excluded from the nation? Why is the ANC so contemptuous of impoverished people?

We are learning new things every day. Part of it I think is that some people in the ANC knew from early on that there would be no real freedom and democracy for the majority. There were compromises from the very beginning, in the negotiations. The demand for land had brought the people of South Africa together but it was compromised from the start. They knew it was freedom for the elites. They accepted that. I don't think it's a mistake that we see so much corruption. Enrichment of the elites was the goal. Cruelty was the method - taking people out of cities at gunpoint to human dumping grounds, the violence of evictions, the repression when people ask to be counted as human beings.

Where does that cruelty, that disrespect for humanity come from?

That's a difficult question. These politicians are also parents, they have daughters, they have sons. How are they so cruel to us while going home to their families every day? At what stage does a politician step out of the garment of the politician and be a human being? This is the same question we ask about the police. At what stage does a police officer step out of his uniform and become a human being?

Look, we have acknowledged that politicians are liars. There is nothing serious that I can discuss with politicians. But if you love your family why can you not think of other people in the same way that you think of yourself and your family? When we have negotiated with them I was trying to find the human being that remains once they shed that garment. I couldn't find a person. I couldn't find a sense of humanity, humility or regret. All I could see in that garment was something like a skeleton. All I found was the opportunistic elements that are left when a person no longer possesses the characteristics of a human being, that care, that consciousness, that willingness to look after other human beings, that fear for what brings shame on someone.

It's a difficult question because you have to be a human being before you can be a politician, before you can be a leader. You can be a professional, you can be whatever, but there are things that should not desert you, there are things that should not happen to you as a human being.

Some people in the ANC feel that for them to be in charge, for them to be leaders, their power must be felt in a physical way. For me to feel that I am in charge, I must be controlling, somebody must feel the pinch that I am in charge. There must be fear. This makes them feel better. It stops them from looking at the emptiness behind the garment.

But fear is not respect.

Leadership becomes the way to control people, it becomes the way to feel empowered because you have this power, I mean physical power to control other people. That's what they enjoy, and for me that goes in hand with the mentality of the colonial time and thinking.

When I grew up in the village there was this thing of being disgraced. You would not want to be disgraced, to disgrace your family. If you were violent to someone, if you stole from someone, you were humiliating your family. You were dehumanising your family, your village.

There are characteristics that constitute a complete human being. A human being ought to have love. A human being ought to have kindness and respect for other people, for the world. But a human being should also have fear, fear of the disgrace that comes from damaging other people. If you are a person that says I don't care what has happened to your consciousness; if you are a person that will harm other people without feeling humiliated, without feeling disgrace then your humanity is slowly, slowly going away from you. You are abandoning your humanity.

There is so much that we have missed as a nation in terms of decolonising our thinking around culture, around leadership, around the nation. You cannot be out there talking about transformation and change when you have not dealt with the colonial damage to yourself. You can't just say now it's 1994, now there's voting, now there's democracy, there's freedom.

It reminds me of how after the war between the UDF and Inkatha there was a realization from the African spiritual perspective, the cultural perspective, to say a lot of people were involved in wars, they have blood in their hands. Some of them were using muthi which really gave them the energy, the enthusiasm to kill, a kind of psychological courage to face guns even if they only had sticks. There was a belief that muti works well when you face the enemy, that the moment you turn your body away you weaken and this causes everyone to be defeated.

It is very dangerous to use the arts of war without developing political consciousness at the same time. There needed to be a conversation, a ritual, some kind of cleansing to move on from that war mentality when the time came for people to assume leadership, to think about building a nation, especially in this province. We cannot just proceed without acknowledging this, and working to undo it, whether in a cultural or spiritual form. It is very dangerous to take power without emancipating yourself, without emancipating yourself from the culture of war, and from colonial oppression. We continue to underestimate the damage that was done during colonial rule, during the war in this province.

Do you think that the violence against migrants has the same roots, that it comes from the damage done by colonialism?

There's no doubt about that. People look at this in a very shallow way. It is not just xenophobia. There are people saying that MK [Jacob Zuma's new political party] is the answer because now the unity of the Zulu people will prevail. I know this thinking from my own experience. When I grew up in a village we were raised as Zulus. We were raised to know that the only people on earth, not even in South Africa, are the Zulus. Our understanding was that any human being is a Zulu. The others are just creatures. It haunts us for the rest of our life from one generation to the other. But once you grow, you realise that not everyone is a Zulu. But we have not had a conversation about this as Zulus, as a nation.

So the politicians want to feel that they have power, to feel stable in the world, to feel that they are someone, and they do that by exercising power, physical power, against us, against the poor and others. Poor people can do the same, they can exercise power against other poor people, people who speak different languages or were born in other countries. We make ourselves feel that we are not weak by being cruel to other people, by having power over them, by hurting them, even killing them.

How has Abahlali built such an ethnically diverse movement and sustained it under intense pressure, a movement in which migrants have been welcomed too? What is the concept of the human that is being built in the movement?

When we talk of ubuntu we have universalised it. It is not the ubuntu we grew up with. I mean people outside always notice you being white, the politicians and the academics. We know you are a human being, we recognise and see a human being.

We can't complain about white supremacy when on the other side we are promoting Zulu supremacy or the supremacy of people born here against migrants. The movement is internationalist.

We have to rework the understanding that we grew up with. We are struggling for our humanity, not just for it to be recognised but also to be more human. There's that deeper question. I guess what makes us sensitive to that, to have so much respect for a human being, is the scars that we all carry, the pain, the burden. Pain. Everyone has pain. We start with everyone's pain. Then we reflect back. Have we been human enough?

The system has been brutal to us but we cannot say that we are resisting it if we are brutal to one another because of a lack of understanding each other's humanity. When we start like this, by recognising each other's pain, it is easy to really centre ubuntu.

One thing we really insist on, one thing that is really important, is our dignity, which is why we put it at the centre of the work that we do. We have so many demands. People are homeless, people are landless. But before we can engage in the struggle for even the most urgent needs of the people we must have properly defined our own world. This is even more urgent.

What will it take to get land? How will we get that land? What will we do with it when we get it? If we get land and the other things that we need without being human, if we have land but we do not have ubuntu . . . Well, can you imagine?

You often speak about becoming human, and losing humanity, as a process.

Yes, it's a process. The fact that your bones are those of a biological human only means that you have the skeleton of a person. It does not confirm your humanity. You may be a skeleton that still needs the process of building, that still needs ubuntu towards yourself, to others, to nature. A human being is incomplete if it is defined in isolation to others.

So is the movement a place where people become more human as well as demanding that the society become more human?

Absolutely. You've got it right. We have to get it right. We have to get it right before we impose, before we demand others to do the same. We have to be the people, human beings before we can make demands for learning other things.

From the beginning I have been struck by how in this movement leaders listen more than they speak. In meetings everyone speaks, you will listen and then only speak at the end.

You look for the points of shared understanding, consensus, not to give a line.

Well of course there is no emancipatory politics without listening. Some people will say it's a skill. But for me listening is much deeper than that. It's about being human, being human together. It's an acknowledgement, an embrace of others. It's not just an embrace of them as you see them, but of how they come through the world to this moment, their suffering, their hopes, their views, how they breathe, how they express themselves. For me that's being human.

As a leader you have to listen to people very carefully, understand their pain, their thinking. You have to learn from them. You already have what you know, but every time you listen to another person you have the opportunity to learn from them. Every person is a world on their own. You can't say that you are on the side of the people, that you are with the people if you don't take them seriously as people. In fact you can't say that you are on the side of the people if you don't take yourself seriously as a person among other people.

Listening is humanistic. We build our humanity through listening.

You cannot listen well if you don't recognise the humanity of the person that is speaking, if you are not open to their thinking, their wisdom. You have to value all the people that are often not valued, the elderly, the so-called uneducated, all the people who nobody wants to listen to. If you fail to do this I don't think you can really be able to meet the people. Willingness to listen, to learn, especially from those who are often not listened to, creates a different set of moral standards, a different kind of politics.

You know when we started our struggle it was always given a meaning from outside. We were always told that we were struggling for 'service delivery'. Well, we have to keep saying that we were not only fighting for water and electricity, that we were also fighting for land, and for a different relationship to the land. But we also had to be clear that people were fighting to be heard, to be listened to.

Many years ago at a meeting in Pietermaritzburg a woman stood up. She cried. She said I have no one. I am a widow. I am a single mother. I have voted. I have a councillor. But I have no one to cry to. We can struggle with her for land and all the other things that she needs to live a dignified life, a life worthy of a human being. But struggle can be long and it can be very hard. But in that moment of the first meeting we can listen to her. And listening can be healing. I learned that listening can be healing. Listening heals the one who speaks and is heard. Of course it also keeps the one who listens human, and so it can be healing for the one who listens too. It stops us from seeing people as objects, as numbers, as instruments.

Before we come to Abahlali we come from divided families, families broken by the long history of oppression, ongoing oppression. The violence, the dispossession, the denial of humanity, well, these things have never stopped for the poor. We all bring our own burdens. Oppression has played itself in different ways. We are raised in different ways. Nobody comes through this society without trauma. We bring all that into the movement. There is a great responsibility to deal with all this within struggle, together. When people bring this into the movement, they don't off load it into the movement, they load it onto the movement. So healing becomes very important.

There has to be an ability, a moment, to acknowledge that what troubles you has been heard, has been processed. For each of us the damage that has been imposed on us needs to be acknowledged.

That's the beginning of the route to healing. You just have to accept what you have, what you bring into the process of healing.

It's not always so much about what a listener will tell you. They'll never have a super word to console you. Healing is a process. You narrate your story, your suffering, to a person who has the ability to listen. The ability to listen is not just about silence and using the ear. There's a particular way in which the expression from the speaker filters into the listener's heart, into their veins. There's power in that, a real power when the person that is narrating, that is expressing, can actually feel that they have connected to the person who is listening, that they have been seen, that they have been heard, that they have been understood.

You have to remember that you are provoking someone's emotions. This has to be taken very seriously. But connection translates into the power of healing. To achieve that connection you don't just listen with your ears. You use your name, you use your heart. That way you build connection and the power for the one who has travelled to feel that I am being taken seriously here. It is not a simple process.

Who listens matters. You are not going to talk to anyone. The movement has a way of choosing its listeners, shaping them.

Colonialism didn't just expropriate land and cattle. It didn't just force people into labour. It also expropriated their right to decide for themselves, to be adults among other adults. The forms of development we have had after apartheid have continued this. Some forms of leftism have continued this. The continuities with the colonial past are not just economic.

Yes, it is a big question. I think that the problem is exactly this. This is why it has become normal for politicians to lie to people. But of course we know that they lie to certain people and they don't lie to certain people. This is because some people count as people and others don't count as people. The logic of colonialism remains.

We have to have a serious conversation around these things. It is going to take time because colonialism took time to install these ideas and to decolonise the mind, well, it will take time. But time on its own will not fix this. You need thinking together in struggle, the power of thought organised and mobilised in struggle.

Sometimes you question the power of education. You question those who are educated. You question the function of institutions of higher learning. Sometimes they may talk about decolonisation but most people come out of university having learnt that they are better than other people, that they should think and speak and decide for other people. Most people do not come out of university with a deeper humanity. Often the main thing for people who have had that educa-tion is to make sure that they are on the other side of the line that separates the rich from the poor. Often they have the same judge-ments about the poor as other middle class or rich people. Of course there are exceptions, people such as Comrade Ruthie [Ruth Wilson Gilmore] and others. These people are able to think together with other people, to think together outside of the university, to share their learning with the people and to learn from the people.

Many people in this movement have suffered for their commit-ment. People have been slandered, assaulted, jailed, tortured, had their homes destroyed, been killed. Many people have serious health issues as a result of years of stress. Many people do not sleep.

Oppression will protect itself ruthlessly. It will protect its sense of superiority, of its right to dominate, ruthlessly. It will always present those who demand to be recognised as human as criminals, as part of some conspiracy, as people who must be crushed to protect society.

Repression is always a lesson. It is meant to tell us to know our place, that we should have known our place. It is meant to teach us that there are limits to what you can say, what you can enjoy, who you can talk to, what you can demand, what value you can give to your life and to the lives of those around you. If you make the mistake of thinking that you are a human being and that you can engage others as human beings, well, then violence is inevitable. It is inevitable that your character will be defamed. If you cross the line and you don't learn the lesson that is given to you then the ultimate price is death.

The message is very clear. Who the hell are you to think that you can take your place in society as a person among other people? Who the hell do you think you are? Know your place. Keep quiet. Vote for the politicians every few years. Attend some NGO workshops. Be good girls and boys.

The price that we have had to pay tells you a very big story about what freedom and democracy have really meant in South Africa.

The courage that people have shown in this struggle is remarkable. Many of the people who have been assassinated knew that they would be killed if they continued to disobey oppression, if they continued to struggle. This courage, this determination, is built and sustained together.

To continue knowing very well that you are playing with fire, knowing very well that you could be killed at any time, having been taught, having being shown that those who behave like you have been killed takes courage.

That courage comes from really being human. It comes from humanity. That courage is as simple as that. It comes from humanity because if you got it right, if you became a human being that comes with responsibilities. And one of those responsibilities of course is courage, courage to cross that line.

If you keep quiet when humanity and dignity are vandalised that troubles your humanity. You have the responsibility to say something, to act. Being a human being is not that you are able to breathe and eat. It comes with responsibility, responsibility to act, even if it means death. The responsibility that comes with being human is as deep as that.

Everyone will die but what's the use of being killed slowly slowly while the meaning you have given to your life, the value that you have given it, rots away?

We have to choose from no choice. Will you honour your life, and the lives of other people, by risking it? Will you confront truth and reality? It is not easy though. It is not just assassinations or the police that take life suddenly. We also die slowly from the diseases that come from stress. That's a long process of having to be killed slowly.

We should not be selfish. We should die knowing the truth, knowing how to better the next generation. We all want freedom in our lifetime but we know the reality that all we are doing is planting the seed to grow into the future, to benefit the generations to come. It's hard to tell if you can enjoy the freedom that you struggle for in this lifetime. You have to trust that the next generation will continue.

But we are here and we must choose whether we relax into oppression, take it as normal, and die slowly slowly, getting into the grave every day or we confront the truth, confront justice and the possibility to die early. At least we can create courage for others to continue the struggle knowing that we may not achieve anything.

I think that we have not been appreciating the importance of creating the space where we can build courage, of being able to say that in the midst of all of this it is important to stand firm and not compromising. Your sense of humanness in the struggle, I think that is what they system is so afraid of. It is afraid of people who want to be brave because they are actually showing others that it is doable, that it is possible in the midst of all this. The system wants to create fear, so much fear that you don't even try.

But if there are people who are brave, who do try, then it gives the possibility for others to do the same, and if there are many who do the same then it threatens the power of the system.

Abahlali changed the old ANC slogan 'Amandla! Ngawethu!' to 'Amandla! Awethu ngenkani!'. Across the country shack settlements are often named eNkanini. Inkani, this stubbornness, with an aspect of forcefulness, has become a very important idea in the struggles of impoverished people, in and out of the movement.

40

When we say 'Awethu ngenkani' it means that we realised that we don't have power without stubbornness, without courage. You have to be brave. There's no way that we can pretend that we are not at war. The struggle is a war.

In war it is mostly men that are expected to fight. The majority of your members are women.

Struggle is a struggle. A fight is a fight. War is war. A lot of war, a lot of violence, is directed at women or makes women worse off. Women are the most affected by war. So without women being in the war, being in the war as women, without women fighting, they are not going to be emancipated. There will be no freedom for them. None of us can escape the fight and there will be no real emancipation for any of us if women are not at the centre of the fight.

The movement is a series of linked meetings, thousands and thousands of linked meetings. That is where people think together. Nelson Mandela, the Mandela of the 1950s, wrote about the prospect of revolutionary democracy based on the consensus seeking meetings he had experienced in the Thembu royal homestead. He did not deal with the fact that these were meetings of men though.

Yes, the way we hold our meetings comes from rural life, from African culture. But even today it is often still difficult for women to participate in these meetings. They will attend the meetings, they can be a majority at the meetings, but sitting on the floor, often on the left hand side, and expected to be quiet. Of course they do have power, but through men. There are often pre-meetings at home. Often when a man speaks vigorously at a meeting you must know that what he says has been influenced or shaped by what women have said at home. A lot of what men say has been influenced by women even if they are full of pride and do not acknowledge this when they speak.

It is different here. We have the same way of holding the meeting, where everyone can speak, where the person running the meetings tries to ensure that everyone can speak, that nobody is overlooked or disrespected, and to try and find consensus. But here women's power is open. Women have all the power to express their views and influence meetings. A majority of our chairpersons, the people running the meetings are women. We are intentional about building the power of women. This is what makes Abahlali so powerful.

South Africa is such a violent society. There is violence among the people. Impoverished people are ruled by state violence. If people organise they are repressed by state and party violence. The movement is armed, of course, for self-defence, but it has always been non-violent. There have been meetings in which women have strongly expressed their opposition to forms of politics with a violent posture or content, and done so as women. The movement will always have large banners opposing violence against women at its big meetings. This question of peace seems to be at the heart of the experiment to develop a different kind of politics.

Yes. Colonialism used violence to dispossess the African people. African people resisted with violence. We all know the names of Makhanda, Bambatha. We fought so many battles. We carry that history. It's the same question that we discussed earlier. This burden, this culture of war, this idea that power is won or lost through war.

Violence comes from this history. Of course Makhanda and Bambatha were political, they were resisting oppression, resisting colonisation. Today the violence from the state and the ANC is to defend oppression. The violence within society is not political. Desperate damaged people are just destroying each other. And these days making people criminal is a big part of how violence gets justified.

Those who were oppressed had to find others to oppress. It is not just the politicians. A man who is disrespected and undermined at work may want to be in charge at home, to feel in charge. He may bring oppression home.

The damage done to us all is expressed in this violence. It has deep roots from the colonial form. And if we ignore that we do not want

42

to confront, if we do not have an honest conversation about healing, about decolonising the mind, about undoing this thinking we will continue to live in this violence, in the politics of blood.

EU Safety Information

Publisher: Daraja Press, PO BOX 99900 BM 735 664 Wakefield, QC J0X 0C2, Canada

info@darajapress.com | https://darajapress.com

EU Authorized GPSR Representative: Easy Access System Europe – Mustamäe tee 50, 10621 Tallinn, Estonia, gpsr.requests@easproject.com

For EU product safety concerns, please contact us at info@darajapress.com

www.ingramcontent.com/pod-product-compliance
Lightning Source LLC
Chambersburg PA
CBHW062105270326
41931CB00013B/3217